THE BREAKING POINT

It is April 1775. Here in Massachusetts, revolution is in the air. British troops are posted in the streets of Boston. Everyone you know is nervous. Fights sometimes break out between colonists and the British redcoats. Fights even break out between colonists who favor independence and those loyal to the British Crown. With all these fights, you can't help but wonder, will war break out too? How did it come to this?

Turn the page.

The tension between Britain and its American colonies has been slowly building for years. King George III began trying to raise money from the colonies back in the 1760s. Britain taxed basic things such as sugar and, with the Stamp Act, all paper documents. They even taxed playing cards.

Colonists insisted they should not have to pay taxes to Britain without having a voice in British government. "No taxation without representation!" was a popular saying. When the Crown pushed forward with the taxes anyway, many colonists resisted. In response to the Stamp Act, mobs marched in the streets and threatened Britain's stamp distributors.

The Townshend Acts of 1767 went even further. They taxed many essentials of daily life such as lead, glass, paint, and tea. Many American business owners agreed to boycott British imports of these products as protest. Others wrecked businesses that

BATTLING FOR A NEW NATION

AT LEXINGTON AND CONCORD

A HISTORY-SEEKING ADVENTURE

by Eric Braun

CAPSTONE PRESS

a capstone imprint

Published by You Choose, an imprint of Capstone
1710 Roe Crest Drive, North Mankato, Minnesota 56003
capstonepub.com

Library of Congress Cataloging-in-Publication Data is available
on the Library of Congress website.

ISBN 9781669069324 (library binding)
ISBN 9781669069294 (paperback)
ISBN 9781669069300 (ebook PDF)

Summary: YOU are living under British rule in the Massachusetts colony in the
1770s. You're sick and tired of Britain's unfair laws and high taxes. You and your
fellow colonists long for independence. When British redcoats march on Lexington
and Concord, will you fight them with your fellow patriots? Or will you remain
loyal to the Crown? Step back in time to face the dangers and decisions that real
people had to make to fight for their independence.

Editorial Credits
Editor: Aaron Sautter; Designer: Bobbie Nuytten; Media Researcher: Jo Miller;
Production Specialist: Whitney Schaefer

Image Credits
Alamy: Album, 86, Ivy Close Images, 46, North Wind Picture Archives, 4, 27, 94;
Getty Images: Balashark, 94, Balefire9, 88, Christine_Kohler, 29, duncan1890, 81,
FPG, 104, Hulton Archive, 18, Interim Archives, 33, 76, Joe Raedle, 41, Lee Snider,
34, NSA Digital Archive, 71, Three Lions, Cover; Shutterstock: A. Emson, 53;
Wikimedia: Missouri History Museum, 63, NARA, 39, New York Public Library -
Digital Collections, 9, The National Guard, 65, 107

Printed and bound in China. PO 5827

TABLE OF CONTENTS

ABOUT YOUR ADVENTURE

YOU are living during a difficult time in American history. Great Britain has put a lot of pressure on the American colonies with unfair laws and high taxes. Many colonists desire independence. But some wish to stay loyal to the Crown.

In 1775, things are more tense than ever. Skirmishes with British troops in Lexington and Concord, Massachusetts, will spark a long and bloody war. How will you respond? Will you be a patriot and fight for the cause of independence? Or will you remain loyal to England?

Turn the page to begin your adventure.

sold British goods and threatened customers who shopped there. At that point, King George began sending troops to the colonies to keep things in order.

In March 1770, a huge brawl broke out in Boston, Massachusetts, between angry patriots and British redcoats. Five colonists were killed and several more were injured in the fight. This event later became known as the Boston Massacre.

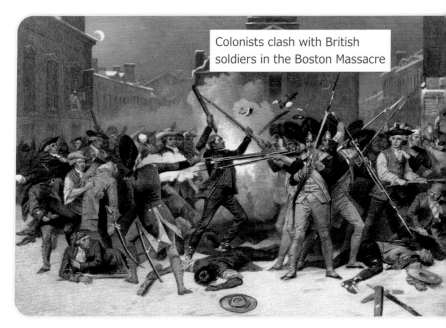

Colonists clash with British soldiers in the Boston Massacre

Turn the page.

Things grew worse in December of 1773. Patriots sneaked onto docked British ships and threw 342 chests of tea into the water. This protest later became known as the Boston Tea Party.

In response to these acts of defiance, Britain sent Thomas Gage to act as the royal governor of Massachusetts. The colony was in rebellion, and Gage's job was to restore peace and order. He took away rights that Massachusetts had long enjoyed, such as the right to self-govern, which only made the tensions worse.

You weren't present for the events that led to the current situation. But you've heard a lot about them. News spreads fast when it comes to revolution. The colonists feel crushed by British taxes, and Boston is crawling with armed British soldiers. The city is like a powder keg and ready to explode.

Gage feels the tension too. To gain an advantage over the colonists, he plans to send troops to Concord, Massachusetts, to seize a stash of weapons that were stolen from the British over the winter. Little does he know that American spies learned of his plan and moved the weapons. Nevertheless, British soldiers will be marching toward Concord soon. When they do, the patriots will be ready.

- To be a farmer trained to fight as a minuteman, turn to page 13.

- To be a tavern owner's wife who is hiding rebel weapons, turn to page 37.

- To be a loyalist asked to spy for the British, turn to page 69.

CHAPTER 2

READY TO FIGHT

You're an independent person, and always have been. As a farmer, you have to be. You built your own home and farm buildings, and when things need repair, you do it. You care for your animals and plant your crops. You manage your land and protect your family. Did King George help you birth your calves? Did the British Crown send troops to rescue you when your horse collapsed in a blizzard? Of course not.

Like many colonists, you believe fiercely that the colonies should be independent from Britain. All Britain offers is high taxes and strict laws— and a royal pain.

Turn the page.

That's why you're a leader in your local militia. You don't just believe in independence—you're willing to fight for it. In fact, you were part of the group of men who stole arms and ammunition from a British fort last winter. The very weapons that Thomas Gage now thinks he's going to take back. Good luck with that, Gage!

You're in bed one night when you hear guns firing and church bells ringing in the distance. Your farm is out in the country, but the noises wake you up. Something is happening.

You get out of bed, kiss your wife, and get dressed. Rifle in hand, you stand on your porch and listen. Soon, you hear something. Not guns or bells, but the *clop! clop! clop!* of a horse's hoofs on the dirt road. It's riding fast. Within minutes, a horseman approaches your farmhouse. Your rifle is loaded, but you wait patiently.

"Hello!" the rider calls in the dark. "I come with news from Samuel Adams!"

You step into the road and greet him as he climbs off his horse. The horse snorts and snuffles, steamy breath billows from its nose.

"It's happening this morning," he says excitedly. He explains that the British troops are marching from Boston at this very moment. They're on their way to Concord where they believe the weapons are stashed.

He tells you that you need to gather the militia and prepare to fight. You could try to stop the British soldiers at Lexington, which is on the way to Concord. Or you can lead the militia to Concord to defend it.

• To meet the British at Lexington, turn to page 16.
• To go to Concord, turn to page 19.

The redcoats will have to march through Lexington to get to Concord. You might as well stop them there.

You ride to another farm down the road to roust one of your men, and then you ride on to another farm. One by one, you gather the "minutemen" of your militia. These are men who can be ready to fight in a minute.

News spreads quickly, and soon you all meet John Parker, the captain of your militia, at a tavern in Lexington. There is excited chattering among the men as you wait for news.

Near dawn, a rider gallops up to the tavern. You and Parker step outside to meet him. "They're coming now," the scout says. "And there are a lot of them."

"Gather the men," Parker says to you. "We'll meet at the town square."

You're not sure what his plan is, but you do as you're told. The militia assembles in the center of town and waits.

In the pale dawn light, you soon see them— hundreds of redcoats marching toward you. You realize the scout was right. You're terribly outnumbered. It would be unwise to engage in a fight with them.

"Disperse!" Parker commands. You and the other men step aside to let the redcoats march by. The two sides face each other, weapons loaded and ready to fire. You can feel that many of your men are nervous. The British are likely nervous too.

Suddenly one of the British units turns toward you. You don't understand what's going on, and you fear someone will start shooting. And then you hear a shot. You're not sure which side it came from.

Turn the page.

Colonists battle British redcoats in Lexington, Massachusetts

Parker yells, "Hold fire!" So does the British captain. But nobody wants to be caught flat-footed, and both sides begin firing at each other. Several of the horses get spooked, and they gallop off with their riders trying to regain control. Gunpowder smoke fills the air, and you can no longer see the British on the other side of the town square. Parker is still shouting to hold your fire, but you can hear musket balls whizzing through the air.

• To return fire toward the British, turn to page 22.
• To retreat behind a stone wall, turn to page 23.

You alert some of the men in your militia and ride with them to Concord, where you meet your leader, Colonel Barrett. Barrett directs you to muster the men on a hill just outside of town with several other militias. It's an impressive sight to see everyone gathered. Your heart fills with pride.

Around 8:00 a.m., you see a line of British regulars marching toward the town. You watch as they march across the North Bridge over the Concord River and enter town. Barrett advises caution. You don't want to get into an unnecessary, bloody fight. After all, the weapons and ammunition they're after are not here.

The British troops fan out through the town, knocking on doors and searching farm fields, taverns, and stores. At one point a fire breaks out in the town.

Turn the page.

"What's that?" grumbles a minuteman named Williams. He's a gunsmith who lives in Concord, and you've known him many years. "Are they burning the town?"

You're not sure, but the fire grows as you watch. Barrett directs you to advance to a lower hill, closer to the town. Fife players and drummers play a jaunty song to inspire your courage and announce your arrival. You approach the North Bridge, which is guarded by a handful of redcoats. When they see your numbers approaching, they retreat into the town. Then some of them start tearing planks out of the bridge.

"They mean to slow us down so they can destroy the town," Williams says. Other men mutter agreement. The men are growing angry.

"Weapons loaded!" Barrett shouts as you draw closer to the bridge.

"Look!" says Williams, pointing toward another road. You turn to see two more militia units coming to join you. Again, you feel a swell of pride. What a show of strength!

That's when a gunshot rings out. There is a brief pause as everyone tries to figure out who fired and where. But then more shots are fired. You kneel and take aim, firing at one of the redcoats on the bridge. You hit him, and he falls. The redcoats begin to retreat in haste!

The redcoats are retreating from the town on their way back to Boston. Your unit should pursue them. But then you notice Williams is lying on the ground. He's bleeding badly.

- To stay behind with Williams, turn to page 25.
- To stick with your unit, turn to page 27.

You are not going to stand around and let yourself get shot. You will fight the hated redcoats! You shoot into the smoke, aiming for the shadowy figures of British soldiers. You quickly reload your rifle.

But your gunshot has attracted the attention of another redcoat, who turns toward you and shoots. You see the fire burst from his barrel, and a split second later you feel a hot, ripping pain in your shoulder. You fall to the ground, bleeding.

Several minutes pass as you lay there in great pain but trying to be quiet. You can only listen as gunshots ring out and men scream in anger or pain. You hope you won't be noticed. Soon the shooting stops. Several redcoats emerge from the smoke, and you see one of them stab a colonist with his bayonet. They don't see you yet. Your rifle is loaded.

- To play dead and hope they leave you alone, turn to page 29.
- To try to shoot one or more redcoats, turn to page 31.

There's a stone wall just a short distance behind you, and you rush there to take cover. Most of your unit joins you there.

You peer over the wall and watch, and eventually the shooting stops. By now, more British officers have shown up. They have a quiet discussion on the green, and then they muster their troops. Soon, they begin to march onward toward Concord.

You climb back over the wall and look around. Captain Parker is standing among the men, assessing the damage. You count eight dead colonists. You look around and see a mix of horror and fury on the faces of the other minutemen. American blood has been shed.

No official war has been declared, but a change has occurred. You're angry. You want revenge.

Turn the page.

The redcoats are all on their way to Concord. It will be several hours while they search for munitions there. Then they'll come back this way on their return to Boston. Parker plans to wait here to confront them.

But you're not sure if you want to stay with him. You have some guns and ammunition hidden at your farm. You don't know if the redcoats will be searching homes outside of Concord. If they find the weapons at your farm, you hate to think what they may do to your wife and children.

- To stay and fight the British when they return, turn to page 32.

- To check on your family, turn to page 34.

The sight of your friend bleeding on the ground takes some of the fight out of you. You decide to stay back and take care of Williams while your fellow colonists pursue the redcoats. You tear off a piece of his shirt and tie it around his wounded leg. Then you help him to his feet. He'll be okay if you can get him home to rest.

You help Williams onto his horse, and the two of you ride to his house in town. His wife opens the door as you approach.

"Oh, no!" she gasps.

"He'll be okay," you say. Williams is too tired to say anything. You help him off the horse and inside. The table is set with dirty teacups and plates with crumbs on them. "Visitors?" you ask.

"The redcoats," she says. "They were looking for arms, but of course we have nothing here. Honestly, they were quite kind."

Turn the page.

She says they were polite to her and her teenage son. They even paid for the tea and cakes they ate.

It's weird to think of kindness coming from these "red devils." As badly as you want independence, you realize that everyone in this conflict is human. You hope that whatever happens in the future, there won't be too much violence.

THE END

To follow another path, turn to page 11.
To learn more about Lexington and Concord, turn to page 101.

Seeing Williams injured only makes you angrier. You promise to return to help him later. Then you pursue the redcoats with your unit.

You follow them at a distance, taking cover in the woods and behind walls. The nervous redcoats continue to march. Finally, someone on your side fires a shot. A British soldier falls to the ground. The redcoats are exposed in the road, while you and the colonists are protected. You also outnumber them.

Turn the page.

Colonists ambush British troops on the road back to Boston

The air is ragged with the noise of gunshots. Through the smoke, you see that you are killing many of the enemy. They keep marching away, faster now, returning fire occasionally. You shoot one, and he falls. You reload. You shoot another, and he falls. Your friends are cheering.

Up ahead is a field of boulders, and as the redcoats approach, more shooting erupts. More rebels are hiding behind the boulders, and more British are going down.

You feel a thrill of victory. But you also feel a small, creeping sense of dread. War is unavoidable now. And although you've won this battle, the British are much better trained and better armed. It will be a long, bloody war. Of that, you are sure.

THE END

To follow another path, turn to page 11.
To learn more about Lexington and Concord, turn to page 101.

If you shoot, you might get one of the British soldiers. But then the others will discover you for sure. If you want to live, your best bet is to play dead.

British soldiers armed with swords and bayonets

Turn the page.

You shut your eyes and hope nobody notices you. You try to steady your breath. You hear the screams of two of your fellow rebels as they are stabbed by redcoats. You're sickened by the terrible sound, and part of you wants to get up and defend your friends. But you know you're outnumbered, and if you get up, you'll be killed. So, you stay perfectly still and quiet.

You're lucky. Either the British don't see you, or they assume you're dead, because they leave you alone. As you lay there listening to your friends dying, you vow revenge. You will fight the British until you are either free—or dead.

THE END

To follow another path, turn to page 11.
To learn more about Lexington and Concord, turn to page 101.

You can see that war is certain at this point. You want to do your part for the cause for independence. Your gun is loaded, so you roll up on your elbows, take aim, and fire. You hit one of the redcoats in the chest, and he screams and falls to the ground.

Seeing this, another redcoat runs toward you. Your gun is empty. Though you're wounded, you manage to scramble to your feet. You swing your rifle's bayonet at the soldier and slice his hip. But it's only a minor cut.

The British soldier hits you in the nose with the butt of his rifle, and pain explodes in your head. You fall to the ground as blood pours from your nose. As you pass out from the pain, you know your fighting days are done.

THE END

To follow another path, turn to page 11.
To learn more about Lexington and Concord,
turn to page 101.

You and your wife have hidden the weapons at your farm. You're confident the British will never find them even if they do stop to search. So, you let your anger rule the day. Your friends lay dead on the ground, and you're going to get revenge.

Over the next few hours, more rebels join you. You have a large force assembled now. Parker directs you to take a position behind some boulders by a bend in the road. Soon you hear the sound of boots tromping on the dirt road.

When the redcoats appear at the bend, you and the other rebels open fire. Some of the enemy scramble for cover, but most run through the gunfire in hopes of getting past you. As you and the other rebels shoot, British soldiers drop to the road one at a time. Finally, the fighting is done. You've barely suffered any casualties. Meanwhile, the British have suffered many.

Colonists take cover behind a stone wall while attacking British soldiers

Against all odds, the rebels seem to have won this battle. One of the rebels lets out a shout of triumph. Everyone is excited but exhausted. You have no doubt that war will be declared now. It will be a long and bloody war. The British have a larger, better-trained army. But you've shown that you can stand against them. You're ready to fight for independence.

THE END

To follow another path, turn to page 11.
To learn more about Lexington and Concord,
turn to page 101.

Thinking of your wife and son at home alone while British soldiers tromp through the farmhouse makes you angry. Even more than the death you've already seen today. So, you mount your horse and gallop home.

When you get there, your wife is waiting out front. "They found two cannons," she says flatly. You had buried them in your rye field. You hate to lose the weapons, but you're more concerned about your family.

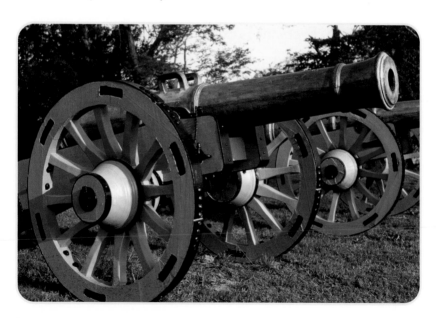

"Are you okay? Where's Jesse?" Jesse is your twelve-year-old son.

"They wanted to arrest him," she says. "But I convinced them he had nothing to do with it. It's lucky you were out, really."

This is true. They would have arrested you. Instead, your whole family is safe. And they only got two cannons. Two cannons are a small loss. And now the redcoats will have to pass through Concord on their way back to Boston. When they do, they'll meet a furious rebel force.

War is certainly looming now. Perhaps it was unavoidable after those weapons were stolen last winter. Now that you've seen bloodshed and real battle, you can only hope it will be worth it.

THE END

To follow another path, turn to page 11.
To learn more about Lexington and Concord,
turn to page 101.

CHAPTER 3

FEMINIST REBEL

You and your husband own a tavern in Concord, Massachusetts. Your family are all very pro-independence. In fact, you're deeply involved in the cause. You've been hiding many of the rebels' weapons in your tavern.

But the weapons are not your only secret. You also write and publish an anonymous political page. In it, you often criticize colonists who are loyal to the Crown. Some of them are "mandamus councilors." They carry out royal laws and report rebel activity.

Turn the page.

These short-sighted scoundrels get especially harsh words in your pages. "They are being bribed by the British at the price of liberty!" you wrote recently.

As a woman, it's risky enough to be writing about politics. That area is meant for men alone. But you're also a feminist. You often write about the subservient role of women in society and compare it to the position of the colonists.

Although your husband is a fierce rebel like you, he doesn't know you publish these pages. Your words can be pretty radical even for independent-minded men. If the British were to discover your identity, they may consider it treason. There's no telling how they would punish you.

One afternoon a horseman arrives at the tavern. "I bring word from Boston," he says. You and your husband invite him to sit at a table, and you serve him something to drink.

"You need to move or hide your weapons," he says even before he sits. "The redcoats know they're in Concord, and Thomas Gage is sending in troops. They'll search every building in town."

Major General Thomas Gage was commander-in-chief of British forces in North America

• To bury the weapons behind the tavern, turn to page 40.
• To move them out of town, turn to page 43.

Your tavern is next to the forest at the edge of town. The thick forest is a perfect spot to hide the weapons. You and your family get to work that very night.

You don't carry lanterns in case any loyalists might be watching. Carrying picks and shovels, you go half a mile into the woods and dig several deep holes.

The next night you get help from some neighbors you trust. Together, you bury several cannons, dozens of rifles and pistols, and many boxes of ammunition.

Then, you wait.

The morning of April 19, another messenger gallops into town with news that the British are on their way.

"There has already been fighting at Lexington. Blood has stained the earth!"

You're shocked and scared. Everyone thought the British would only be searching for weapons, nothing more. But now blood has been shed. Tensions are high among the townspeople.

British soldiers soon cross the North Bridge into town and begin their search, building by building. As they do, your husband and sons leave to join the local militia, leaving you alone.

Turn the page.

When the redcoats finally reach your door, you say, "We're closed! Go away!"

The leader pulls out a pistol and says, "You will let us in now, by order of the Crown!" The other soldier holds a rifle.

You let them in, and the one with the pistol says, "Where are the guns? We know they're here."

"We have nothing," you say calmly.

"You do not have *nothing*!" the one with the pistol says. "We know what you have. Now show us."

How could they know? Someone must have been spying on you.

- To give up a few weapons and keep the rest secret, turn to page 45.

- To deny you have any, turn to page 47.

It's too risky to keep the weapons in town. If the British believe the arms are here, they won't stop until they find them. So, you move everything to a farm far outside town owned by an ally.

Over the next week, you, your husband, the farmer, and a few other rebels work by night to transport and bury cannons, rifles, ammunition, and gunpowder in the farmer's field. The farmer disguises the field to look like it's been freshly planted with wheat.

Then one day in April, another messenger arrives in town. He announces that the redcoats are coming—and there has been fighting in Lexington. Men on both sides have been killed.

"The red devils!" your oldest son, Jed, says.

Monty, the younger son, says, "We have to stop them!"

Turn the page.

"The local militia is heading out to confront them on the road," your husband says. "We won't let them into town."

"Hold on, boys!" you say. "We should stick with the plan. Stay here. Let them search. They won't find anything And then they'll leave. It's too dangerous to fight."

"It's already dangerous, Ma," says Jed. "They've been shooting."

You don't want your husband and sons to fight—it's too dangerous. Plus, you'd be home alone when the British do come. On the other hand, you understand their anger. You feel it too.

- To try to convince them to stay home, turn to page 49.
- To let them go fight, turn to page 51.

"Okay," you say. "Follow me."

You lead the soldiers to a mound of dirt at the edge of your property. They take shovels from your shed and dig up two cannons.

"Two cannons?" says the leader, the one with the pistol. "Where's the rest?"

"That's all we have," you say.

The leader doesn't believe you. He directs the soldiers to search your tavern and the grounds surrounding it, but they don't find anything else. Finally, they give up, and you let out a sigh of relief.

"Let's drag them into the street," the leader says, referring to the cannons. The soldiers take them to the road in front of your tavern. They then use your shovels to smash the transom and wheels. Finally, the leader sets fire to the pile of broken wood. The fire crackles and whips in the wind.

Turn the page.

British soldiers burning canon carriages at Concord

As the two redcoats walk away, wind blows some leaves into the fire. The burning leaves then fly toward the fence along your property, setting a small blaze. You realize the fire could quickly get out of control. You could try to control it yourself. Or you could ask the British soldiers to help.

• To ask the redcoats to help you, turn to page 53.
• To try to handle it yourself, turn to page 55.

"I told you, we don't have any weapons here," you say.

"You're lying," says the one with the pistol. "Our spies have seen British munitions here."

"You've got your information wrong," you say, but the soldiers ignore you and begin searching the tavern. The one with the rifle searches the grounds outside while the leader searches inside. He knocks on walls, looking for hollow hiding spots. He checks the floorboards. Soon he finds a loose board and pries it up. Your heart races.

"Don't!" you say. But it's too late. He lowers himself into the dark space. You hear him shuffling through papers. When he climbs back out, he has several copies of your anti-Crown writings in hand. A bolt of fear shoots through you. What will happen now?

Turn the page.

"It appears your husband is a traitor," he says. For a split second you're angry that he assumes your husband wrote the papers. Of course, he can't imagine that a woman would be smart enough to write and publish them. But then the fear returns. They could arrest your husband.

You think fast. You could deny knowing who wrote them and lie about where they came from. Or you could admit that you wrote them and hope they go easy on you.

- To lie about the papers, turn to page 57.
- To admit to writing them, turn to page 59.

"I need you here," you tell your husband and sons. "When the redcoats come, I can't be alone here. I'll be in danger."

The boys look to their father. Your husband relaxes his angry jaw for a moment and looks at you with soft eyes. "The boys will stay," he says. "But I must go."

Not long after he leaves, two redcoats arrive and search the tavern. You expected them to be cruel "red devils." Instead, they are polite and careful not to damage anything. When they find nothing, they apologize for bothering you.

"Onto the Williams farm, then," says one of the soldiers, and they head toward the door. The Williams farm is where you moved the stash of weapons. Do they know the guns are there? You can't let them find the weapons—it's a huge stash. Losing them would be a blow to the rebellion.

Turn the page.

"The rebels are advancing on the North Bridge, sir," says the other soldier. They both peer out the doorway toward the bridge. Sure enough, a growing number of militiamen are approaching the bridge.

Part of you just wants these soldiers out of your house. If they find your anti-Crown writings, you could be in big trouble. But at the same time, you can't let them search the Williams farm.

- To try to delay them, turn to page 61.
- To get them out of your hair, turn to page 63.

It's your husband and sons' duty to report to the militia. They might be needed to defend the city. "Fine," you say to them. "You'd better go then."

Less than an hour later, two redcoats arrive at the tavern to search for hidden weapons. Finding nothing, they sit at one of the tables and ask for something to drink. You bring them some wine, and they ask for food. So, you feed them, and they eat heartily.

"Wonderful meal," says one of the soldiers, and he pays you for the food and drink. They leave, and you are left alone.

When you go to bed that night, your husband and sons still aren't home. But near dawn, you hear them on the front porch, and you get up.

"We routed them red devils all the way back to Boston!" your oldest son says, grinning.

Turn the page.

The three of them are dirty, tired, and very happy. You fix them a meal and listen to their stories. In the end, very few arms were seized by the British in Concord. And the rebels chased them back to Boston, battling all the way. Many more redcoats were shot than colonists. It sounds like the day was a big success for the rebels.

It also sounds like war will be declared now. There's no turning back. The fighting will be terrible, you know that. But you're glad. You look forward to doing whatever you can to help the colonies gain independence.

THE END

To follow another path, turn to page 11.
To learn more about Lexington and Concord,
turn to page 101.

"Help!" you call out after the British soldiers.

They turn back and see the fire, which is heading toward a general store next to your tavern. They run back.

"Where's water?" the leader asks.

You point to a horse trough beside the tavern. They begin carrying buckets to the fire. The leader calls to some other British soldiers, and they help by carrying water from the Concord River.

Turn the page.

Soon, the townspeople join in, too. The fire rages for a brief period, but in the end little damage is done.

"Thank you," you say to the soldier with the pistol. "What is your name?"

"McHenry," he says, doffing his cap. You chat for a few minutes. McHenry tells you about his children back home in England. He talks about his wife, whom he loves. Finally, he and his partner leave.

You still desire independence, and you will continue to fight for it with your published papers. But a little bit of the hate has died in your heart.

THE END

To follow another path, turn to page 11.
To learn more about Lexington and Concord,
turn to page 101.

You rush to the horse trough by your tavern and grab a bucket. You fill it and dash back to the quickly spreading fire. You toss the water on the leaves, and they hiss and smoke. Meanwhile, the fence is burning higher.

The owner of the general store next to your tavern comes out with his own bucket and helps you. Soon, other townspeople are joining in. The flames on the fence lick the eaves of the tavern, and soon the roof is smoking.

Eventually, you and the townspeople get the fire under control. But you lose part of the tavern. You'll have to close it while your family makes repairs, which means lost income.

Later, you learn that the rebel militias saw the growing fire from a hill outside the city. It appeared to be out of control, so they thought the British were burning down the city.

Turn the page.

They marched down and attacked the redcoats at the North Bridge, resulting in many lost lives. Perhaps if you'd asked the redcoats for help, the fire wouldn't have gotten so big. Then the battle at the bridge wouldn't have happened. Lives could have been saved.

But then the war for independence wouldn't be fought, either. Perhaps the fire at your tavern is a small price to pay for freedom.

THE END

To follow another path, turn to page 11.
To learn more about Lexington and Concord, turn to page 101.

"I found those papers and got them off the street!" you say, thinking fast. "You should be thanking me! I'm trying to find the traitor who wrote them."

"Likely story," says the leader. He has his pistol out again and is pointing it at you. "Why should I believe you?"

"I'm a loyalist!" you blurt. "That's why you didn't find any weapons here. The rebel ideas in those papers disgust me."

He appears to think for a moment, though he keeps his pistol pointed at you. "Our spies have identified this tavern as friendly to the rebels," he says.

"We put on an act," you say. "There are many rebels in town. We all live close together, many of them are my friends—in spite of their treasonous ideas.

Turn the page.

"You don't know how hard it is to live like this. You never know who's a spy, who's for independence, or who is for the Crown."

"Oh, yes . . . I'm sure it's hard," he says.

You're not sure if he's mocking you, but he holsters his gun. He and the other soldier burn your papers in the fireplace, and then they leave. You're safe for now, but you know you'll have to be even more careful from now on. The eyes of the Crown are sure to be watching you.

THE END

To follow another path, turn to page 11.
To learn more about Lexington and Concord, turn to page 101.

You've had enough of these soldiers. You're fed up with the British in general, and you're sick of hiding who you are. So, you straighten up and look the leader in the eye.

"Yes, they're mine," you say. "I write and publish them. Go ahead and read it. Maybe you'll learn something."

The soldiers take you from the tavern and put you on a horse. You all join the other redcoat soldiers and start on your way to Boston.

"You will face charges of treason for these brazen writings!" the soldier says to you.

You're in the middle of dozens of soldiers on horseback and on foot. As you ride on the horse, you go over your defense arguments in your mind. However, after crossing the North Bridge, everything changes.

Turn the page.

A volley of gunshots explode from the hill above. You look over and see hundreds of rebel militiamen coming toward you. The redcoat in front of you slumps over on his horse, shot dead. A foot soldier falls just ahead of him.

You lean down as close to your horse as you can, hoping to make yourself a small target. Bullets rain down, and the army begins moving faster to escape the ambush.

Suddenly the soldier who arrested you falls off his horse. He lays in the dirt with a bleeding stomach. Looking up, the first person he sees is you.

"Help me," he says.

- To give him medical attention, turn to page 65.
- To make a run for it, turn to page 67.

"It's a long way to that place," you say. "Why don't you have some cakes before you go? I made them fresh this morning."

"Why, yes," says the soldier with the pistol. "Right kind of you."

They sit at the table again, and you and your sons take your time serving them. The longer you can delay them, the better. You offer them some wine, and they accept. An hour passes, and soon you hear gunshots going off near the north end of town.

"Fighting at the bridge!" says a soldier in the street.

The two soldiers at your table get up and grab their weapons. Thanking you, they run out to join their army at the North Bridge. You smile, knowing that you prevented them from finding the weapons at the Williams farm.

Turn the page.

Later that day, before the militiamen return from battle, you talk with some of the women in town. You learn that many of them took the same actions you did. They stalled and delayed the redcoats. Some of them lied and misdirected them. It wasn't just you who saved the revolution today. It was many women.

You return to the tavern and light a lantern. While you wait for your husband to return, you begin writing your next political pamphlet. The subject is the strength and importance of women in the fight for independence.

THE END

To follow another path, turn to page 11.
To learn more about Lexington and Concord, turn to page 101.

You glance at your son Jed and see that his anger is welling over. He has always had a strong hatred toward the "red devils," as he calls them. You're worried his temper may get him in trouble. So, you let the redcoats leave.

After they're gone, Jed grabs his rifle and a bag of musket balls.

"What do you think you're doing?" you ask harshly.

Flintlock musket

Turn the page.

"I have to go fight," he says. "The search is over—you'll be safe. If I don't fight, I'll never forgive myself."

"Me too," says Monty, copying his big brother.

Your family is strongly pro-independence and you're all angry at the British. But your sons' intensity right now surprises you. You realize you can't stop them. They're old enough to make their own decisions. As they head out, you can only hope they return alive.

THE END

To follow another path, turn to page 11.
To learn more about Lexington and Concord,
turn to page 101.

Patriots fight British redcoats at the North Bridge in Concord

None of the other redcoats are stopping to help their fellow soldier. They're all running for their lives. You can't just let the man suffer. So, you dismount, take off your apron, and tie it around his wound to try to stop the bleeding. Musket balls whiz all around. You're terrified, but you try to calm the bleeding soldier.

Turn the page.

Soon, two redcoats come with a litter to carry the soldier. They load him onto it and carry him off. They must not know that you were a prisoner.

You scramble away in the chaos of the running men and horses and then hide behind a boulder at the side of the road. You listen to the shooting and the screams of wounded and dying men. It's horrible. You're too scared to look. You sit behind the boulder, trying to stay calm until the commotion finally dies down.

When you finally come out, you walk past dead bodies and blood-stained earth on your way home. Now that you've seen such gruesome war up close, you're no longer sure that freedom is worth this price. But something tells you it is only going to get worse.

THE END

To follow another path, turn to page 11.
To learn more about Lexington and Concord, turn to page 101.

The soldier was going to have you arrested and tried for treason. He's the enemy. Besides, he has other soldiers around who can help him. So, you climb off the horse and start running.

Musket balls fly through the air, whistling as they go. You head for the side of the road to get away from panicked horses and soldiers. But you soon feel a hot sting in your neck.

Your first thought is that it's a bee sting, but it's much more painful than that. As you fall to your knees in the dust, you realize you've been shot. Was it a redcoat trying to keep you from escaping? Or an errant rebel shot? You fall forward onto your stomach. It doesn't matter whose bullet it was. It did what bullets do. It killed you.

THE END

To follow another path, turn to page 11.
To learn more about Lexington and Concord,
turn to page 101.

CHAPTER 4

LOYALIST AND SPY

It's a confusing time. In Concord, Massachusetts, where you live, rebels and loyalists live amongst one another. You figure it's the same way in most of the American colonies. There are no clearly drawn lines showing who is who. No one posts a sign outside their home saying "Loyalist" or "Rebel." You don't know who to trust—or who not to trust.

In the past few months, you've lost your best friend, Hoss Anderson. He's a rebel, and because you're a loyalist, he won't talk to you anymore. What makes it worse is that he's married to your sister Sarah.

Turn the page.

Hoss and Sarah say they are patriots, but you have to laugh at that. After all, you live in a British colony. You're the one who's loyal to the established government. Isn't that patriotism?

The Crown helps protect you, and Britain provides traditions and goods to make life comfortable and interesting. Sure, you wish the taxes were lower. But as a general store owner, you're grateful for the imported tea and other goods that you sell in your store.

One day in March someone knocks on your door. It's two men dressed in the fashionable clothes of city dwellers. You don't recognize them as locals. "May we come in?" says the short one.

You invite them in, and they look around carefully for a moment. Then the short one informs you that they're officers in the British army. They've disguised themselves so they can scout the town.

"We understand you're a loyalist," he says. "We'd like your help."

"What can I do?" you say. You aren't in a militia and you don't have much money. You're not sure how you can help.

"You can observe your neighbors," he says. "Stick your nose into their business."

Now you understand. He wants you to spy on the rebels.

- To agree to spy on your neighbors, turn to page 72.
- To say no, turn to page 74.

"I'm willing," you say. "What are you looking to find out?"

The short man smiles and takes a seat at your table. The taller one joins him. He rubs the stubble on his chin and then speaks up. "Did you hear about Fort William and Mary?" he asks.

"Of course," you say. Last December, a band of rebels rowed out to the off-shore fort and stole a large number of arms and ammunition. It was an outrageous crime.

"Our network of spies informs us that the stash is here in Concord," says the tall one, rubbing his chin again. "We'd like to know exactly where. And who's responsible."

"Any information you can provide about who in town is loyal would also help," adds the short one. "When we come back for the weapons, we may need food or lodging."

You agree to find out what you can, and they leave. That afternoon you go to visit Hoss and Sarah at their home, which is connected to Hoss's blacksmith shop. You bring some wine and bread from your shop as a peace offering.

They let you in, but they seem wary. You share a snack and talk about things unrelated to politics—family, crops, business at your shop. It's nice to spend time with family and not argue.

You hope they feel the same way. And, as the day turns to night, you sense that they're softening a bit. This might be a good time to try to get information out of them.

- To ask if they know anything about stolen weapons, turn to page 76.
- To play it cool and just snoop around, turn to page 78.

"I'm sorry," you say. "I'd truly love to help, but my family already hates me. And with all the rebels around here, it doesn't feel safe."

The two men try to convince you. At one point you think they may even threaten you. But finally, they give up and leave.

Six weeks later, the British army arrives in Concord and begins searching homes and businesses one by one. Again, two men arrive at your door. These men are in uniform, and one of them is injured.

"What happened?" you say as you help him inside. You lay the man on your bed and get him some water.

"Fighting at Lexington," says the other soldier. "And there's going to be more. The rebels are gathering outside town."

Even as he says this, you hear gunfire outside. It sounds like it's coming from the North Bridge. The fighting has begun.

You get some clean cloth from your store to care for the injured man. His friend decides to stay with him. You clean and bandage the man's wounds. Then you feed both men. Before long, there's another knock at your door. It's your sister, Sarah.

"Hoss has been shot!" she says urgently. "I need your help."

She'll be furious if she sees the redcoats in your home. But she's family, and she needs your help.

• To let her in, turn to page 80.
• To say you'll meet her at her house, turn to page 82.

The best way to get information is to ask, right?

"Say, do you remember when those rebels stole weapons from the British fort?" you ask, casually.

Colonists were often angry with those loyal to the Crown.

"Sure," Hoss says slowly. He shifts in his seat and looks at you hard.

"I was just thinking how hard it would be to hide all that," you say.

"I wouldn't know anything about that," Hoss says.

"Of course," you say. "I was just wondering if you'd heard anything. You know, just curious."

"Just curious?" Sarah says. "You never cared before. Why so curious now?"

"I saw those men at your house the other day," Hoss says. "You're working for the Crown, aren't you?"

- To deny it, turn to page 85.
- To try to get them to see your side, turn to page 87.

Hoss and Sarah will never tell you anything. And you'd rather avoid a fight if you can. Your best bet is to find out what you can on your own.

After eating, Hoss goes outside to feed the chickens while Sarah washes the dishes. While they're busy, you peek into the blacksmith shop. In the back corner, there appear to be two large crates covered in blankets. You lift a corner of one blanket, but you don't see any markings on the crate. They're nailed shut, but you have a hunch that they contain weapons.

The British army comes to town in April to search for and seize the weapons. Small groups of soldiers fan out through the town. Before long, three soldiers step onto your porch.

Two of them are the same men who visited you before. They're joined by a younger man with pimply skin and a rifle. All three are excited by the fighting they've already seen today. You have a feeling they're eager for more. The younger one makes a fist and nods to you. "How can you live in the same town with these filthy rebels?"

"Never mind that, Boris," says the leader. Then he turns to you. "What have you learned for us?"

You had planned to tell them about the crates you found. But suddenly, the thought of soldiers storming into your sister's home feels very uncomfortable. What if they arrest Sarah and Hoss? Or hurt them? On the other hand, if you don't give them any information, they might take their frustrations out on you.

• To tell them about the crates, turn to page 90.
• To keep the information to yourself, turn to page 93.

"Let me get you some clean linens," you say, leading your sister inside.

She steps in but freezes when she sees the two redcoats. She says nothing, but you can see her neck turning red and her jaw tighten. You hurry into the store and return with the linens, bandages, and soap. She thanks you quietly and leaves quickly.

After she's gone, the healthy soldier stands up and looks you over. "Rebels," he finally says. "You're helping rebels. Maybe *you* are a rebel."

You shake your head. "She's my sister. That's all."

"Whose husband was wounded fighting against the Crown."

The wounded soldier sits up. His injury has stopped bleeding, and he seems strong enough to leave. But he's in no hurry to do so.

Minutemen line up to stop British soldiers in Concord

Outside, you can hear guns firing and people yelling. Just down the road, Hoss may be dying. He may need your help. The longer these redcoats stay in your home, the more you worry. You and your sister disagree about independence. But you still love her. You don't want to lose her.

"More water," says the injured soldier.

• To tell the soldiers to leave, turn to page 96.
• To get the wounded man some water, turn to page 98.

"Go home and give him something to drink," you whisper to Sarah. "I'll be there in a moment."

"Can't you come now?"

"I need a moment," you say. "Please."

She gives you a confused look, but she turns and heads home. You gather clean linens and other supplies from your shop.

"I'll be right back," you say to the soldiers. The healthy one just shrugs.

When you arrive at Sarah's home with the supplies, you see that Hoss has a bad gunshot wound in his belly. He lays on the bed breathing heavily.

You help him the best you can, but he dies within the hour. Your sister lays over his body crying.

"I'm sorry," you whisper, rubbing her back.

"Leave me alone," she says through her tears. "I can't stand to look at you, you *loyalist*." She won't lift her head or look at you.

You stand there stupidly for another moment, and then you walk home. The two soldiers are still in your home. The one who was hurt is now sitting up in your bed drinking tea. The other one is relaxing by the fireplace.

They look content—even the injured one. Hoss is dead and your sister hates you. And these two redcoats are here, lounging happily in your home and drinking your tea.

"How much longer will you be here?" you ask.

As before, the healthy one shrugs. Anger wells up in your stomach. You realize you hate them. You feel a change happen inside you.

Turn the page.

You're starting to see the rebels' point of view. The British don't care about you or your family. Maybe you'd be better off without them. Maybe you'll start helping the rebel cause.

THE END

To follow another path, turn to page 11.
To learn more about Lexington and Concord, turn to page 101.

"No!" you say fiercely. You try to look shocked at the accusation. "Never!" you add.

"I don't believe you," Hoss says. "You're a loyalist and a spy for the Crown. You're a traitor to your own family!"

Over the next few weeks, you learn just how many of your neighbors are rebels. People stop shopping at your store, and you're on the verge of going out of business.

When the British come to town in April to search for the weapons, they find a few muskets used for hunting, but nothing more. The stash of weapons was moved a long time ago.

In the following months, more battles take place between the British and American rebels. That winter you close your shop and move to Boston. The city is controlled by the British, so it should be safe there for loyalists.

Turn the page.

Boston, Massachusetts, under British control

It's a long, cold, and lonely journey. You worry about being caught by rebels. The wind lashes your face, and the horse seems to move more and more slowly as snow swirls in the air. You think of Hoss and Sarah. You hope that someday you'll be able to regain their trust and love. You already miss them.

THE END

To follow another path, turn to page 11.
To learn more about Lexington and Concord,
turn to page 101.

You decide it's best to tell the truth. Perhaps they'll understand if you tell them what happened.

"It's true," you say. "Two soldiers came to my home. They asked me to be a spy for them. I didn't think I had a choice. I was afraid. I'm sorry."

"You're sorry?" Hoss says, standing. Because he's a blacksmith, his arms are big and strong. You can see the muscles moving in his forearms as he clenches his fist. You step backward.

"Please understand," you plead. "They intimidated me!"

"I'll intimidate you," Hoss says, and he punches you in the mouth.

You see flashes of light as you stumble back. You scramble to your feet and swing at him, but he grabs your hand. He hits you hard in the face again, and you fall to the floor. Blood drips from your mouth and nose.

Turn the page.

"Get out," he growls.

You are only too glad to obey. You scramble to your feet and run home, where you load your pistol and sit at the table. You're worried that Hoss or another rebel will come to finish you off. But nobody comes.

Flintlock pistol

Eventually you go to bed, still holding your gun. Maybe it was wrong to spy on your family. But Hoss didn't have to beat you so badly. He and the other rebels are so bent on their cause, they will hurt anyone.

As you drift off to sleep, still holding your pistol, you make yourself a promise. You'll continue spying for the Crown. But you'll be sneakier from now on. When the British come looking for information, you'll be happy to provide it.

THE END

To follow another path, turn to page 11.
To learn more about Lexington and Concord, turn to page 101.

The pimply kid is gripping his rifle tightly. His bayonet gleams in the lantern light. You decide you need to get these redcoats out of your store as soon as possible. So, you tell them about Hoss's blacksmith shop and the two suspicious crates.

"I didn't see inside them," you add. "But they look like rifle boxes."

"Is that all?" the leader asks.

"I'm afraid so," you say. "It seems most of the weapons have been moved out of town."

The leader's mouth tightens into a firm line. He's angry, but nods. Then the three of them leave. Only after they've left do you allow yourself a moment to think about what will happen to Hoss and Sarah. You hope they moved the crates out.

That afternoon, a fire fight erupts at the North Bridge. The redcoats suffer many casualties. In fact, the rebels harass them all the way back to Boston. After closing the shop that evening, you go down the road to see Sarah. She answers the door, crying. "Hoss is dead," she says.

You see his body on the bed behind her. A horrible shock runs down your spine and you feel sick to your stomach. "What happened?" you finally utter.

"Some redcoats ransacked the shop," she says between sobs. "The red devils broke open some crates looking for guns. When they saw that the crates held only tools, they destroyed the shop in anger. Hoss tried to stop them, and one of them stabbed him with his bayonet."

Turn the page.

You don't know what to say. You hug her as tightly as you can. "I'll help you clean up. I'll put the shop back together." It won't make up for betraying her, but it's all you can think to do right now. You'll have to live the rest of your life knowing you caused the death of your sister's husband—and your best friend.

THE END

To follow another path, turn to page 11.
To learn more about Lexington and Concord, turn to page 101.

You don't want to anger these soldiers. But it would be even worse for them to get angry with Sarah, especially while Hoss is out fighting. So, you shake your head.

"This town is clean," you say. "The rebels moved every last musket ball."

The leader steps very close to you and puts his pistol to your head. "Liar!" he spits.

You try to control your trembling by making your hands into fists. "I wish I was lying," you say. "But it's true. I found nothing."

The short soldier turns to the teenager. "Boris, see if you can jar his memory."

The teen struts over and hits you in the mouth with the butt of his rifle. You collapse onto the floor, blood streaming from your mouth. You spit two teeth onto the floor. "I'm sorry," you say. "You can search the whole town."

Turn the page.

Boris kicks you in the face, and you pass out. When you wake up, it's late at night and the soldiers are gone. Struggling through the pain, you clean yourself up and go to bed. The next morning some loyalists come to your shop. They tell you about the fighting that occurred and the rebels' victory.

Angry colonists sometimes mocked and beat loyalists before running them out of town.

The next few days are slow at the shop—suspiciously slow. It takes you a while to figure it out. But you eventually realize that only loyalists are shopping here. The rebels have boycotted you. They may know that you spied for the Crown.

Even Sarah and Hoss are avoiding you. You want them to know that you didn't tell the redcoats anything. But then you would have to admit that you were spying. You'll have to be satisfied with knowing that you chose your family over the Crown. When the war really starts, you'll have to choose again. And the stakes may be even higher.

THE END

To follow another path, turn to page 11.
To learn more about Lexington and Concord, turn to page 101.

"I need to go," you say. "I'd like you to leave too."

"We'll decide when we leave," the healthy soldier says. "Now get him some water. And get me some tea."

You hesitate, and the healthy soldier stands up, pointing his bayonet at you. "I don't want to ask again," he says.

"Actually, I'll take some of that wine over there," says the soldier in your bed. You realize he's not badly hurt at all. These men are just taking advantage of you. You begin to panic. Will they ever leave?

"No!" you shout. "I've helped you. I have helped the Crown. But you must leave—now."

The soldiers exchange a glance. You've angered them. Your heart races as you think of what they might do. They could shoot you.

Instead, the healthy soldier walks to your cabinet and serves himself and his friend a drink. They have no intention of leaving. So you make a bold decision. You hurry out the door.

You rush to Sarah and Hoss's home. Sarah won't speak to you, as she's angry about the redcoats, but she lets you inside. You take care of Hoss and don't say much yourself. You and Sarah have had many arguments over the years. You always make up in the end. As long as Hoss is fine, you believe that the three of you will become close again.

THE END

To follow another path, turn to page 11.
To learn more about Lexington and Concord, turn to page 101.

You figure you have little choice. You can't make the soldier leave—it's the royal army. So, you do as they ask. You give them water, and when they ask for wine and food, you fix them a meal.

They don't leave until late that evening. It seems that their goal was to hide out here and avoid the fighting. You're disgusted with them, and you slam the door behind them when they leave.

When they're finally gone, you quickly gather some bread and dried meat. You run down to Hoss and Sarah's home, hoping you're not too late to help Hoss. You're angry with yourself for not standing up to those greedy redcoats. You wonder if Sarah will ever forgive you. If Hoss is dead, you may never forgive yourself.

THE END

To follow another path, turn to page 11.
To learn more about Lexington and Concord, turn to page 101.

CHAPTER 5

IGNITING THE WAR FOR INDEPENDENCE

In 1763, Britain won the French and Indian War, in which it successfully defended its North American colonies from French expansion. However, the long conflict was expensive for Britain. It needed money, and King George III looked to the colonies to provide it. For the British, it made sense that the Americans should help pay the cost for defending them.

King George imposed heavy taxes on many British goods, including sugar, glass, tea, and every piece of paper the colonists used. But the colonies had no voice in British government. They had no chance to debate or dispute the taxes. So, the Americans protested fiercely.

Britain responded by sending troops to Massachusetts and appointed Thomas Gage as royal governor of the colony. Many colonists favored independence and were willing to fight the British for it. They already belonged to militias and were trained to fight.

However, others were loyal to the British. "Rebels" and "loyalists" lived among one another. Life was tense. Neighbors and family members often fought and argued with each other.

By April 1775, rebellion felt unavoidable. Gage decided to seize a stash of weapons and powder that were being stored in Concord.

But the Americans had spies among the British. They learned of the plan and had the weapons moved from Concord into nearby towns.

On April 18, American leaders learned that the British would be marching that night. Several messengers, including Paul Revere, rode through the night to bring a warning to residents throughout the area.

Fighting broke out early in the morning in Lexington, a small town between Boston and Concord. The rebels were heavily outnumbered. They'd been ordered to let the redcoats pass, but a shot was fired anyway. No one knows which side fired first, but it triggered a skirmish. The result was eight dead militiamen and no dead British.

The British then went on to Concord. They found very few weapons there, and they burned what they found.

Paul Revere rides to Lexington to warn colonists about the British

The fire got mildly out of control, which alarmed the militiamen nearby. They thought the redcoats were burning down the town. They hurried into town to confront the redcoats at the North Bridge.

A British soldier fired first, but this time the rebels had greater numbers. The rebels fired back, and the British retreated.

The redcoats began to march back toward Boston as the militiamen followed them. Angered by the rebel deaths in Lexington, they soon attacked the British again. They fired from behind walls, trees, and buildings. The redcoats fled, and many dropped their weapons.

When they reached Lexington, there were more rebels awaiting them there. The fighting continued nearly all the way back to Boston, with the British taking many more casualties than the rebels.

The Battles of Lexington and Concord saw nearly 300 redcoats killed, wounded, or missing. The colonists had only 95 casualties. The colonists had proven that they could stand up to the British. By the following summer, the war for independence would officially be underway.

The Battles of Lexington and Concord Timeline

April 18, evening: About 700 British troops leave Boston for Concord. Rebel messengers Paul Revere and William Dawes ride by horseback to alert rebels in the area.

April 19, 5:00 a.m.: British troops reach Lexington, where about 70 militiamen wait for them. A shot is fired. Nobody knows who fired it. The British open fire on the colonists, killing eight and wounding more. Then the redcoats move on toward Concord.

April 19, 8:00 a.m.: The British arrive in Concord, where about 400 rebels await them. About 220 redcoats secure the North Bridge while the rest search the town. They burn the few weapons and ammunition they find.

April 19, 9:00 a.m.: Rebels on the hill think the British are burning the town, so they advance on the North Bridge. Fighting breaks out there. The British decide to retreat to Boston. The colonists fire on them as they go.

April 19, mid-morning: The British reach Lexington again, where the rebels who were attacked earlier that morning fire on them. The redcoats are continually ambushed by rebels on the journey back to Boston.

Lexington and Concord Casualties

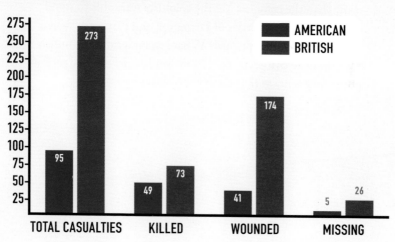

AMERICAN
BRITISH

	TOTAL CASUALTIES	KILLED	WOUNDED	MISSING
AMERICAN	95	49	41	5
BRITISH	273	73	174	26

Other Paths to Explore

1. Colonists in favor of independence, known as "rebels," and those in favor of loyalty to the British, known as "loyalists," lived together in communities throughout the colonies. Sometimes friends and families were on opposite sides of this fierce, emotional conflict. How would it feel to argue or fight with loved ones over something so important?

2. Think about life as a colonist during the 1770s. What do you think life would be like having to pay the heavy British taxes? Do you think it was fair for the American colonies to pay the cost of defending them in the French and Indian War? Why or why not? Would your answer change if the colonies were represented in the British government?

3. The British had a larger, more experienced, and better-trained army than the colonies. Yet the colonists were able to stand up to them in the Battles of Lexington and Concord. Why do you think this happened? What advantage did the militias have over the British troops? How would it feel to face such a powerful enemy at that time?

Select Bibliography

Borneman, Walter R. *American Spring: Lexington, Concord, and the Road to Revolution.* New York: Little, Brown and Company, 2014.

Daughan, George C. *Lexington and Concord: The Battle Heard Round the World.* New York: W. W. Norton & Company, 2018.

History.com: Battles of Lexington and Concord
https://www.history.com/topics/american-revolution/battles-of-lexington-and-concord

History.com: Townsend Acts
https://www.history.com/topics/american-revolution/townshend-acts

Glossary

bayonet (BAY-uh-net)—a long metal blade attached to the end of a musket or rifle, used to stab enemies

independence (in-dih-PEN-duhnss)—freedom from the control of other people

loyalist (LOI-uh-list)—a colonist who was loyal to Great Britain during the Revolutionary War

militia (muh-LIH-shuh)—a group of volunteer citizens who are trained to fight, but serve only in an emergency

minutemen (MIH-nuht-men)—colonists who were ready and willing to fight at a moment's notice

munitions (myoo-NIH-shuhns)—materials used to wage war, including weapons and ammunition

rebel (REH-buhl)—an American colonist who fought for American independence from Britain

representation (reh-preh-zen-TAY-shuhn)—the right to have someone act on behalf of and be the voice for a group of people in government

tax (TAKS)—money collected from a country's citizens to help pay for running the government

transom (TRAN-suhm)—a horizontal crosspiece that connects the two sides of the base of a cannon

Read More

Boutland, Craig. *What Happened at Lexington and Concord?* New York: Rosen Publishing, 2024.

Braun, Eric. *Enduring Winter at Valley Forge: A History-Seeking Adventure.* North Mankato, MN: Capstone, 2024.

Haugen, Brenda. *The Split History of the Battles of Lexington and Concord.* North Mankato, MN: Compass Point Books, 2018.

Internet Sites

American Battlefield Trust: Lexington and Concord
battlefields.org/learn/revolutionary-war/battles/lexington-and-concord

Ducksters: American Revolution: Battle of Lexington and Concord
ducksters.com/history/battle_of_lexington_and_concord.php

National Park Service: Minute Man National Park
nps.gov/mima/index.htm

JOIN OTHER HISTORICAL ADVENTURES WITH MORE
YOU CHOOSE SEEKING HISTORY!

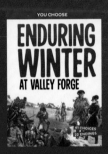

YOU CHOOSE

ENDURING WINTER
AT VALLEY FORGE

41 CHOICES
22 ENDINGS

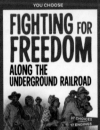

YOU CHOOSE

FIGHTING FOR FREEDOM
ALONG THE UNDERGROUND RAILROAD

37 CHOICES
17 ENDINGS

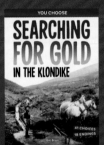

YOU CHOOSE

SEARCHING FOR GOLD
IN THE KLONDIKE

41 CHOICES
18 ENDINGS

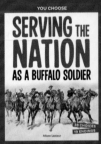

YOU CHOOSE

SERVING THE NATION
AS A BUFFALO SOLDIER

38 CHOICES
19 ENDINGS

About the Author

Eric Braun is the author of dozens of books for young readers on topics ranging from sports and history to fractured fairy tales and middle grade fiction. Besides stories, he loves bike riding, camping, adventures, and wearing hats. Learn more at heyericbraun.com.